NBA CHAMPIONS

CHICAGO BULLS

AARON FRISCH

CREATIVE EDUCATION

Published by Creative Education
P.O. Box 227, Mankato, Minnesota 56002
Creative Education is an imprint of The Creative Company
www.thecreativecompany.us

Book and cover design by Blue Design (www.bluedes.com)
Art direction by Rita Marshall
Printed by Corporate Graphics in the United States of
America

Photographs by Getty Images (Randy Belice/NBAE, Andrew
D. Bernstein/NBAE, Nathaniel S. Butler/NBAE, Jonathan
Daniel, John Iacono, Manny Millan/Sports Illustrated,
Adam Jones, Heinz Kluetmeier/Sports Illustrated, Fernando
Medina/NBAE, Joe Murphy/NBAE, Paul Natkin/WireImage,
Robert Abbott Sengstacke, Rick Stewart)

Library of Congress Cataloging-in-Publication Data

Frisch, Aaron.
Chicago Bulls / by Aaron Frisch.
p. cm. — (NBA champions)
Includes bibliographical references and index.
Summary: A basic introduction to the Chicago Bulls
professional basketball team, including its formation in 1966,
great players such as Michael Jordan, championships, and
stars of today.
ISBN 978-1-60818-132-2
1. Chicago Bulls (Basketball team)—History—Juvenile
literature. I. Title.
GV885.52.C45F75 2011
796.323'640977311—dc22   2010050664

CPSIA: 030111 PO1448

First edition
9 8 7 6 5 4 3 2 1

Cover: Derrick Rose
Page 2: Michael Jordan
Right: Norm Van Lier
Page 6: Ben Gordon

TABLE OF CONTENTS

Chicago has some of the biggest skyscrapers in America

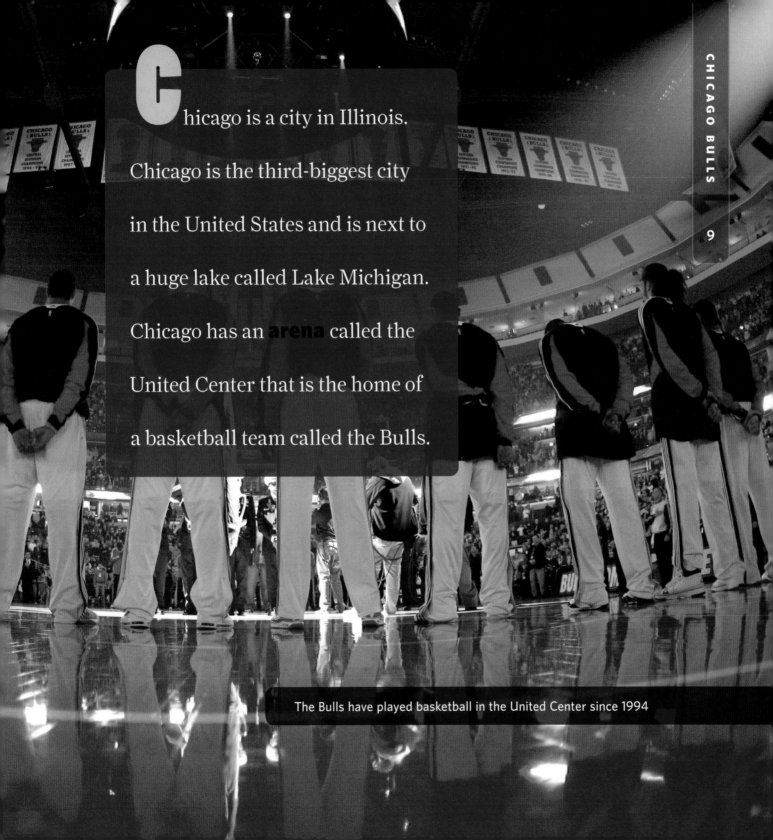

Chicago is a city in Illinois. Chicago is the third-biggest city in the United States and is next to a huge lake called Lake Michigan. Chicago has an **arena** called the United Center that is the home of a basketball team called the Bulls.

The Bulls have played basketball in the United Center since 1994

The Bulls are part of the National Basketball Association (NBA). All the teams in the NBA try to win the **NBA Finals** to become world champions. The Bulls play many games against teams called the Bucks, Cavaliers, Pacers, and Pistons.

Bob Love joined Chicago in 1968 and played there for eight seasons

The Bulls started playing in 1966 and made the **playoffs** their very first season. Fans cheered for players like high-scoring forward Bob Love. But the Bulls could not get to the NBA Finals.

Teams had to use several players to defend against Michael Jordan

The Bulls had some bad seasons in the early 1980s. But in 1984, they added star guard Michael Jordan. When the Bulls hired smart coach Phil Jackson, they became almost unstoppable. The Bulls won the NBA championship in 1991, 1992, and 1993!

BULLS FACTS

- Started playing: 1966

- Conference/division: Eastern Conference, Central Division

- Team colors: red, black, and white

- NBA championships:

  1991 — 4 games to 1 versus Los Angeles Lakers

  1992 — 4 games to 2 versus Portland Trail Blazers

  1993 — 4 games to 2 versus Phoenix Suns

  1996 — 4 games to 2 versus Seattle SuperSonics

  1997 — 4 games to 2 versus Utah Jazz

  1998 — 4 games to 2 versus Utah Jazz

- NBA Web site for kids: http://www.nba.com/kids/

Guard Ron Harper helped Chicago win titles in 1996, 1997, and 1998

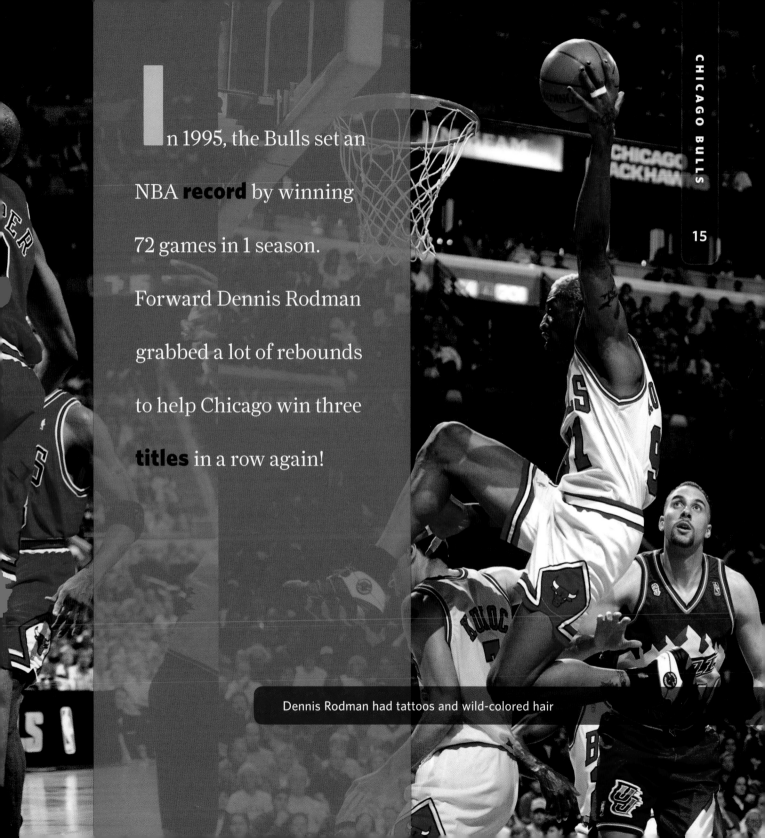

In 1995, the Bulls set an NBA **record** by winning 72 games in 1 season. Forward Dennis Rodman grabbed a lot of rebounds to help Chicago win three **titles** in a row again!

Dennis Rodman had tattoos and wild-colored hair

Why Are They Called the Bulls?
In the 1800s, people used to trade and sell cows and bulls in Chicago. Bulls are male cattle. They are powerful animals that have horns.

Chicago did not win any more championships after that. The Bulls added so many new, young players that people called them the "Baby Bulls." Fans soon were cheering for players like forward Joakim Noah.

Joakim Noah became the Bulls' best rebounder by 2010

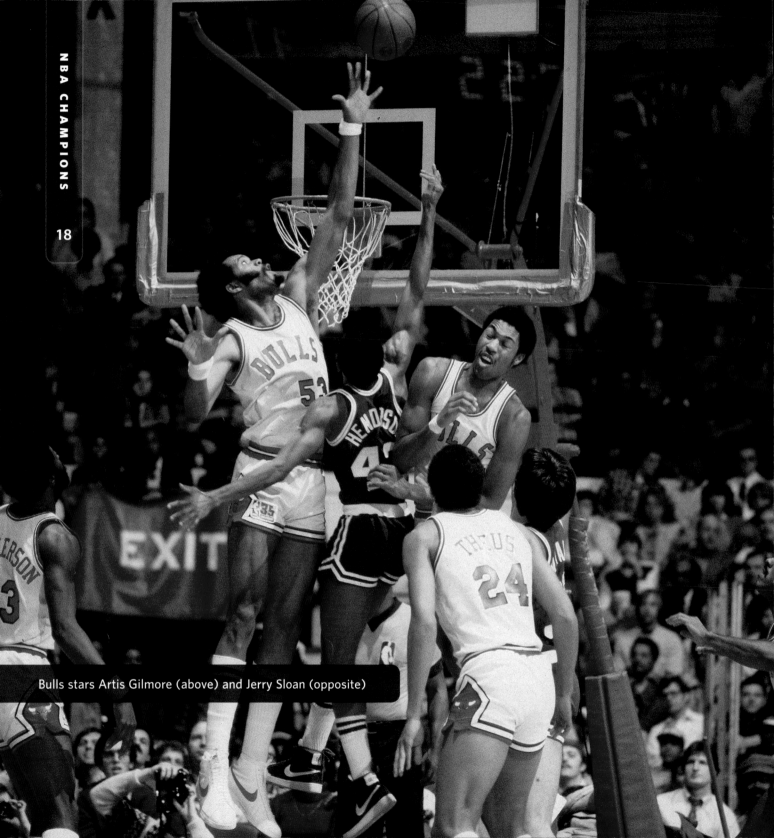

Bulls stars Artis Gilmore (above) and Jerry Sloan (opposite)

Chicago has had many stars. Jerry Sloan was a tough guard who played tight defense. He later became a good NBA coach. Artis Gilmore was a big center who was very strong. He was nicknamed "The A-Train."

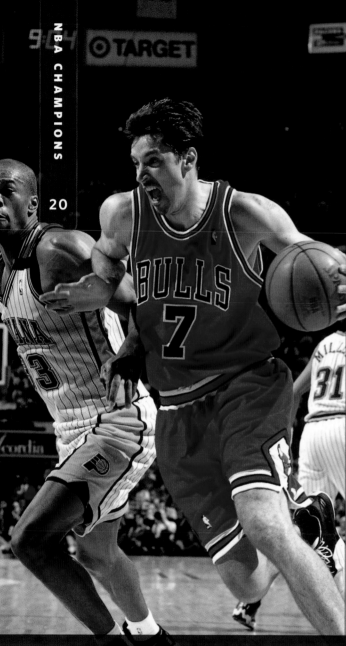

Toni Kukoc was 6-foot-11 and had a good shooting touch

Scottie Pippen joined the Bulls in 1987. He was a fast forward who played very well with Michael Jordan. Bulls forward Toni Kukoc was one of the first NBA stars from Europe.

SAY IT LIKE THIS

Kukoc
KOO-kohch

Scottie Pippen leaped high for dunks and also played tough defense

In 2011, Derrick Rose won an award as the NBA's best player

In 2008, the Bulls added point guard Derrick Rose. He was quick and good at giving out **assists**. Chicago fans hoped that he would help lead the Bulls to their seventh NBA championship!

GLOSSARY

arena — a large building for indoor sports events; it has many seats for fans

assists — passes that let a teammate quickly score a basket

NBA Finals — a series of games between two teams at the end of the playoffs; the first team to win four games is the champion

playoffs — games that the best teams play after a season

record — something that is the most or best ever

titles — another word for championships

INDEX